Baby Animals in the Wild!

Lion Cubs in the Wild

by Marie Brandle

Bullfrog Books

Ideas for Parents and Teachers

Bullfrog Books let children practice reading informational text at the earliest reading levels. Repetition, familiar words, and photo labels support early readers.

Before Reading
- Discuss the cover photo. What does it tell them?

- Look at the picture glossary together. Read and discuss the words.

Read the Book
- "Walk" through the book and look at the photos. Let the child ask questions. Point out the photo labels.

- Read the book to the child, or have him or her read independently.

After Reading
- Prompt the child to think more. Ask: Lion cubs play. What does it help them learn to do?

Bullfrog Books are published by Jump!
5357 Penn Avenue South
Minneapolis, MN 55419
www.jumplibrary.com

Library of Congress Cataloging-in-Publication Data

Names: Brandle, Marie, 1989– author.
Title: Lion cubs in the wild / by Marie Brandle.
Description: Minneapolis, MN: Jump!, Inc., [2023]
Series: Baby animals in the wild!
Includes index. | Audience: Ages 5–8
Identifiers: LCCN 2022010083 (print)
LCCN 2022010084 (ebook)
ISBN 9798885240741 (hardcover)
ISBN 9798885240758 (paperback)
ISBN 9798885240765 (ebook)
Subjects: LCSH: Lion—Infancy—Juvenile literature.
Classification: LCC QL737.C23 B72475 2023 (print)
LCC QL737.C23 (ebook)
DDC 599.757—dc23/eng/20220317
LC record available at https://lccn.loc.gov/2022010083
LC ebook record available at https://lccn.loc.gov/2022010084

Editor: Eliza Leahy
Designer: Molly Ballanger

Photo Credits: dalhethe/iStock, cover; Eric Isselee/Shutterstock, 1, 3, 10, 19, 22, 23bm, 24; BirdImages/iStock, 4; Andrey Skaternoy/Shutterstock, 5, 23tl; Henk Bogaard/Shutterstock, 6–7; GP232/iStock, 8–9; Reto Buehler/Shutterstock, 11, 23tm; Stu Porter/Shutterstock, 12–13; earleliason/iStock, 14–15, 23bl; Hel080808/Dreamstime, 16–17; Dennis Stogsdill/iStock, 18, 23tr; DELFINO Dominique/Hemis/SuperStock, 20–21; Maciej Czekajewski/Shutterstock, 23br.

Printed in the United States of America at Corporate Graphics in North Mankato, Minnesota.

Table of Contents

Part of the Pride

A lion roars.

Why?

cub

She guards her cubs.

The cubs can't walk yet.
Mom carries them!

They drink Mom's milk.

They grow.

**Their fur has spots.
The spots go away
as they grow up.**

spot

Mom grooms them.

She licks their fur.

11

They learn to walk.

Then they run!

They join the pride.

They live on the savanna.

pride

meat

Mom hunts.

She brings meat
to the cubs.

They eat.

They play.
They pounce.
This helps them
learn to hunt.

They learn to roar!

They grow up.
They have cubs
of their own!

Parts of a Lion Cub

What are the parts of a lion cub? Take a look!

ear

fur

tail

mouth

leg

paw

claw

Picture Glossary

cubs
Young lions.

grooms
Cleans.

pounce
To jump forward and grab something suddenly.

pride
A group of lions.

roars
Makes a loud, deep sound.

savanna
A flat, grassy plain with few or no trees.

Index

To Learn More

FACT SURFER

Finding more information is as easy as 1, 2, 3.

❶ Go to www.factsurfer.com

❷ Enter "lioncubs" into the search box.

❸ Choose your book to see a list of websites.